crochet
your own
dolls
& accessories™

Contents

Bella Ann

SKILL LEVEL

INTERMEDIATE

FINISHED SIZE

Doll: Approximately 13 inches tall

Umbrella: 5 inches around x 5 inches high

MATERIALS

- Red Heart Soft Yarn medium (worsted) weight yarn (5 oz/256 yds/ 140g per skein): **4 MEDIUM**
    - 3 oz/154 yds/84g each #2515 turquoise, #9388 wheat and #4600 white
    - 2 oz/102 yds/56g each #4420 guacamole and #6768 pink
    - 1 oz/51 yds/28g #1882 toast
- Size G/6/4mm crochet hook or size needed to obtain gauge
- Tapestry needle
- 2 small black beads
- 4-inch piece of cardboard
- Blush
- Cotton swab
- 5 small buttons
- Polyester fiberfill
- 12-inch chenille stem
- Stitch marker

GAUGE

Unstuffed: 9 sc = 2 inches; 11 sc rows = 2 inches

Stuffed: 12 sc = 3½ inches; 20 sc rows = 4 inches

PATTERN NOTES

Warning: Doll is not intended for children under 3 years of age.

Work in continuous rounds. Do not join or turn unless otherwise stated.

Mark first stitch of round. Move marker as work progresses.

For umbrella, always change colors in last stitch worked. Carry unused colors loosely across back of work.

Weave in ends as work progresses.

DOLL

FIRST LEG 4

Foundation rnd: With white, ch 2, 6 sc in 2nd ch from hook, **do not join** (see Pattern Notes). **Mark first st** (see Pattern Notes).

Rnd 1: 2 sc in each sc around. (12 sc)

Rnds 2–7: Sc in each sc around.

Rnd 8: 2 dc in each of next 3 sc, sc in each of next 9 sc. (6 dc, 9 sc)

Rnd 9: 2 dc in each of next 6 dc, sc in each of next 9 sc. (12 dc, 9 sc)

Rnd 10: [**Sc dec** (see Stitch Guide) in next 2 dc] 6 times, sc in each of next 9 sc. (15 sc)

Rnd 11: [Sc in each of next 3 sc, sc dec in next 2 sc] 3 times (heel). Start to stuff with fiberfill, and continue to stuff as you go. (12 sc)

Rnds 12–19: Sc in each sc around, **changing colors** (see Stitch Guide) to wheat in last st of last rnd. Fasten off white.

Rnd 20: With wheat, sc in **back lp** (*see Stitch Guide*) of each st around.

Rnds 21–34: Sc in each sc around. At end of last rnd, fasten off.

2ND LEG
Follow directions for First Leg, changing colors to white in last st of last rnd. Fasten off wheat.

BODY

Rnd 1: Sc in each sc around 2nd Leg, sc in each sc around First Leg, making sure both feet are pointing in same direction. (*24 sc*)

Rnd 2: Sc in back lp only of each sc around.

Rnd 3: [Sc in next sc, 2 sc in next sc] around. (*36 sc*)

Rnds 4–11: Sc in each sc around. Stuff with fiberfill.

Rnd 12: [Sc in each of next 4 sc, sc dec in next 2 sc] around. (*30 sc*)

Rnd 13: [Sc in each of next 3 sc, sc dec in next 2 sc] around. (*24 sc*)

Rnds 14–23: Sc in each sc around.

Rnd 24: Sc in each of next 5 sc, ch 12, sc in 2nd ch from hook and in each of next 10 chs (*first strap*), sc in each of next 17 sc of rnd 23, ch 12, sc in 2nd ch from hook and in each of next 10 chs (*2nd strap*), sc in each of next 2 sts of rnd 23, changing to wheat in last st. Fasten off white.

Rnd 25: Sk straps, working in back lps, sc in each sc around. (*24 sc*)

Rnds 26 & 27: Sc in each sc around.

Rnd 28: [Sc in each of next 2 sc, sc dec in next 2 sc] around. (*18 sc*)

Rnd 29: *Sc in each of next 5 sc, [sc dec in next 2 sc] twice, rep from * once. (*14 sc*)

Rnd 30: [Sc dec in next 2 sc] around (*neck*). (*7 sc*)

Rnd 31: 2 sc in each sc around. (*14 sc*)

Rnd 32: Rep rnd 31. (*28 sc*)

Rnds 33–40: Sc in each sc around.

Rnd 41: [Sc in each of next 3 sc, sc dec in next 2 sc] 4 times, sc in each of next 8 sc. (*24 sc*)

Rnd 42: [Sc in each of next 2 sc, sc dec in next 2 sc] around. (*18 sc*)

Rnd 43: [Sc in next st, sc dec in next 2 sts] around. Leaving 5-inch end, fasten off and stuff. *(12 sc)*

Weave end through top of sts on last row, pull to gather top of head closed. Secure end.

ARM
Make 2.

Foundation rnd: With wheat, ch 2, 6 sc in 2nd ch from hook, do not join. Mark first st.

Rnd 1: Sc in each sc around. *(6 sc)*

Rnd 2: [Sc in next sc, 2 sc in next sc] around. *(9 sc)*

Rnd 3: Sc in each sc around.

Rnd 4: 2 hdc in each of next 2 sc, sc in each of next 7 sc. *(4 hdc, 7 sc)*

Rnd 5: Hdc in each of next 4 hdc, sc in each of next 7 sc.

Rnd 6: [Sc dec in next 2 hdc] twice, sc in each of next 7 sc *(hand)*. *(9 sc)*

Rnds 7–25: Sc in each sc around. Fill Arm with stuffing as you go, leaving last ½ inch of Arm unstuffed.

Leaving 5-inch end, fasten off. Hold edges tog. Working through both thicknesses, sew across top to close.

FINISHING
With wheat, sew Arms to sides of Body with thumbs pointing forward as shown in photo. With white, sew straps over shoulders to back edge of underwear.

HAIR & FACE
With toast, wrap yarn 135 times around cardboard. Cut lps on 1 side only.

Start at neck and work, row by row, upward toward crown *(see photo)*, tie yarn pieces around each individual st, making sure to knot tightly. Trim as needed.

For face, sew 2 black beads for eyes and apply blush to cheeks with cotton swab as shown in photo.

ACCESSORIES
RAINCOAT
BODY
Row 1: With turquoise, ch 25, 3 dc in 3rd ch from hook, sc in each of next 21 chs, 3 dc in last ch, working in rem lps on opposite side of foundation ch, sc in each ch across, turn. *(44 sc, 6 dc)*

Row 2: Ch 1, working in **front lps** *(see Stitch Guide)*, 4 sc in first sc, sc in each of next 21 sc, 4 sc in next sc, leaving rem sts unworked, turn. *(29 sc)*

Rows 3 & 4: Ch 1, sc in each sc across, turn.

Row 5: Ch 1, sc in each of next 5 sc, 3 sc in each of next 5 sc, sc in each of next 9 sc, 3 sc in each of next 5 sc, sc in each of next 5 sc, turn. *(49 sc)*

Row 6: Ch 1, 2 sc in first sc, sc in each of next 4 sc, sk next 15 sc *(armhole)*, [sc in each of next 2 sc, 2 sc in next sc] 3 times, sk next 15 sc *(armhole)*, sc in each of next 4 sc, 2 sc in last sc, turn. *(24 sc)*

Row 7: Ch 1, [sc in next sc, 2 sc in next sc] across, turn. *(36 sc)*

Rows 8–30: Ch 1, sc in each sc across, turn.

Row 31 (WS): Ch 1, sl st in **back lp** (see Stitch Guide) only across to last sc, 3 sc in last sc, **do not turn**.

Row 32 (WS): Working up side to form the button band, sc in end of each of next 27 rows, working in rem lps of row 3, sl st in each st across, 3 sc in end of row 3, working down other open side of Raincoat, sc in end of each of next 27 rows, turn.

Row 33: Ch 1, sc in each of next 12 sc, [ch 4, sc in each of next 4 sc] 4 times, ch 4, sc in last sc. Leaving rem sts unworked, fasten off.

SLEEVE
Rnd 1: Join turquoise with sc to armhole, sc in each sc around. (15 sc)

Rnds 2–15: Sc in each sc around.

Rnd 16: Sl st in each sc around. Fasten off.

Rep in rem armhole.

FINISHING
Sew buttons to button band corresponding to button loops. Tack down corners of collar, if necessary.

RAIN HAT
Foundation rnd: With turquoise, ch 2, 6 sc in 2nd ch from hook, do not join. Mark first st.

Rnd 1: 2 sc in each sc around. (12 sc)

Rnd 2: [Sc in next sc, 2 sc in next sc] around. (18 sc)

Rnd 3: [Sc in each of next 2 sc, 2 sc in next sc] around. (24 sc)

Rnd 4: [Sc in each of next 3 sc, 2 sc in next sc] around. (30 sc)

Rnd 5: [Sc in each of next 4 sc, 2 sc in next sc] around. (36 sc)

Rnds 6–9: Sc in each sc around.

Rnd 10: Working in **front lps** (see Stitch Guide), [sc in each of next 5 sc, 2 sc in next sc] around. (42 sc)

Rnd 11: [Sc in each of next 6 sc, 2 sc in next sc] around. (48 sc)

Rnd 12: [Sc in each of next 7 sc, 2 sc in next sc] around, join with sl st in first sc. Fasten off. (54 sc)

RAIN BOOT
Make 2.

Rnd 1: With guacamole, ch 9, sc in 2nd ch from hook and in each of next 6 chs, 3 sc in last ch, working in rem lps on opposite side of foundation ch, sc in each of next 6 chs, 2 sc in last ch. (18 sc)

Rnd 2: [2 sc in next sc, sc in each of next 6 sc, 2 sc in next sc, sc in next sc] twice. *(22 sc)*

Rnd 3: [2 sc in each of next 2 sc, sc in each of next 8 sc, 2 sc in each of next 3 sc, sc in each of next 8 sc, 2 sc in next sc. *(28 sc)*

Rnd 4: Working in **back lps** *(see Stitch Guide)*, sc in each sc around.

Rnd 5: Hdc in each of next 3 sc, sc in each of next 10 sc, hdc in each of next 4 sc, sc in each of next 10 sc, hdc in next sc.

Rnds 6 & 7: Hdc in each of next 3 hdc, sc in each of next 10 sc, hdc in each of next 4 hdc, sc in each of next 10 sc, hdc in next hdc.

Rnd 8: Hdc in each of next 3 hdc, sc in each of next 10 sc, [**sc dec** *(see Stitch Guide)* in next 2 hdc] twice, sc in each of next 10 sc, hdc in next hdc.

Rnd 9: Hdc in each of next 3 hdc, sc in each of next 4 sc, [sc dec in next 2 hdc] 7 times, sc in each of next 4 sc, hdc in next hdc.

Rnds 10–18: Sc in each sc around.

Rnd 19: Working in **front lps** *(see Stitch Guide)*, sc in each sc around, join with sl st in first st. Fasten off.

UMBRELLA
LINING
Foundation rnd: With pink, ch 2, 6 sc in 2nd ch from hook, do not join. Mark first st.

Rnd 1: 2 sc in each sc around. *(12 sc)*

Rnd 2: [Sc in next sc, 2 sc in next sc] around. *(18 sc)*

Rnd 3: [Sc in each of next 2 sc, 2 sc in next sc] around. *(24 sc)*

Rnd 4: [Sc in each of next 3 sc, 2 sc in next sc] around. *(30 sc)*

Rnd 5: [Sc in each of next 4 sc, 2 sc in next sc] around. *(36 sc)*

Rnd 6: [Sc in each of next 5 sc, 2 sc in next sc] around. *(42 sc)*

Rnd 7: [Sc in each of next 6 sc, 2 sc in next sc] around. *(48 sc)*

Rnd 8: [Sc in each of next 7 sc, 2 sc in next sc] around. *(54 sc)*

Rnd 9: [Sc in each of next 8 sc, 2 sc in next sc] around. *(60 sc)*

Rnd 10: [Sc in each of next 9 sc, 2 sc in next sc] around. Fasten off. *(66 sc)*

BODY
Rnd 1: With guacamole, ch 2, 6 sc in 2nd ch from hook, 2 sc in each of next 2 sc, **change color** *(see Stitch Guide and Pattern Notes)* to pink, 2 sc in each of next 2 sc, change color to turquoise, 2 sc in each of next 2 sc, change to guacamole. *(12 sc)*

Rnd 2: [Sc in next sc, 2 sc in next sc] twice, change to pink, [sc in next sc, 2 sc in next sc] twice, change to turquoise, [sc in next sc, 2 sc in next sc] twice, change to guacamole. *(18 sc)*

Rnd 3: [Sc in each of next 2 sc, 2 sc in next sc] twice, change to pink, [sc in each of next 2 sc, 2 sc in next sc] twice, change to turquoise, [sc in each of next 2 sc, 2 sc in next sc] twice, change to guacamole. *(24 sc)*

Rnd 4: [Sc in each of next 3 sc, 2 sc in next sc] twice, change to pink, [sc in each of next 3 sc, 2 sc in next sc] twice, change to turquoise, [sc in each of next 3 sc, 2 sc in next sc] twice, change to guacamole. *(30 sc)*

Rnd 5: [Sc in each of next 4 sc, 2 sc in next sc] twice, change to pink, [sc in each of next 4 sc, 2 sc in next sc] twice, change to turquoise, [sc in each of next 4 sc, 2 sc in next sc] twice, change to guacamole. *(36 sc)*

Rnd 6: [Sc in each of next 5 sc, 2 sc in next sc] twice, change to pink, [sc in each of next 5 sc, 2 sc in next sc] twice, change to turquoise, [sc in each of next 5 sc, 2 sc in next sc] twice, change to guacamole. *(42 sc)*

Rnd 7: [Sc in each of next 6 sc, 2 sc in next sc] twice, change to pink, [sc in each of next 6 sc, 2 sc in next sc] twice, change to turquoise, [sc in each of next 6 sc, 2 sc in next sc] twice, change to guacamole. *(48 sc)*

Rnd 8: [Sc in each of next 7 sc, 2 sc in next sc] twice, change to pink, [sc in each of next 7 sc, 2 sc in next sc] twice, change to turquoise, [sc in each of next 7 sc, 2 sc in next sc] twice, change to guacamole. *(54 sc)*

Rnd 9: [Sc in each of next 8 sc, 2 sc in next sc] twice, change to pink, [sc in each of next 8 sc, 2 sc in next sc] twice, change to turquoise, [sc in each of next 8 sc, 2 sc in next sc] twice, change to guacamole. *(60 sc)*

Rnd 10: [Sc in each of next 9 sc, 2 sc in next sc] twice, change to pink, [sc in each of next 9 sc, 2 sc in next sc] twice, change to turquoise, [sc in each of next 9 sc, 2 sc in next sc] twice, change to guacamole. *(66 sc)*

Rnd 11: Hold Lining and Body with WS tog and Body on top, with guacamole, working in back lps only of both thicknesses, sc in each st around.

Rnds 12 & 13: Sc in each sc around.

Rnd 14: [Sc in each of next 9 sc, sc dec in next 2 sc] 6 times. *(60 sc)*

Rnd 15: [Ch 4, sk next sc, sc in next sc] around, join with sl st to next sc. Fasten off.

HANDLE
Fold the chenille stem in half and set aside.

Row 1: With pink, ch 30, sc in 2nd ch from hook and in each ch across, turn. *(29 sc)*

Row 2: Ch 1, sc in each sc across. Leaving 18-inch end, fasten off.

FINISHING
Wrap Handle around chenille stem and use end to sew seam. Sew 1 end securely to center of the Umbrella Lining and fold other end into a hook. ❖

Dani Rae

SKILL LEVEL

■■■□
INTERMEDIATE

FINISHED SIZE
Doll: Approximately 13 inches tall

MATERIALS
- Red Heart Soft Yarn medium (worsted) weight yarn (5 oz/256 yds/140g per ball):
    3 oz/154 yds/84g #9388 wheat
    2 oz/102 yds/56g each #4422 tangerine and #9522 leaf
    1 oz/51 yds/28g each #9114 honey and #9275 paprika
- Bernat Satin medium (worsted) weight yarn (3½ oz/200 yds/100g per ball):
    1 oz/46 yds/22g #04615 banana
- Size G/6/4mm crochet hook or size needed to obtain gauge
- Tapestry needle
- 2 small black beads
- Blush
- Cotton swab
- ¼-inch-wide ribbon: 1 yd orange or color of choice
- Polyester fiberfill
- Stitch marker

GAUGE
Unstuffed: 9 sc = 2 inches; 11 sc rows = 2 inches

Stuffed: 12 sc = 3½ inches; 20 sc rows = 4 inches

PATTERN NOTES
Warning: Doll is not intended for children under 3 years of age.

Work in continuous rounds. Do not join or turn unless otherwise stated.

Mark first stitch of round. Move marker as work progresses.

Weave in ends as work progresses.

DOLL
FIRST LEG
Foundation rnd: With wheat, ch 2, 6 sc in 2nd ch from hook, **do not join** (see Pattern Notes). **Mark first st** (see Pattern Notes).

Rnd 1: 2 sc in each st around. (12 sc)

Rnds 2–7: Sc in each st around.

Rnd 8: 2 dc in each of next 3 sc, sc in each of next 9 sc. (6 dc, 9 sc)

Rnd 9: 2 dc in each of next 6 dc, sc in each of next 9 sc. (12 dc, 9 sc)

Rnd 10: [Sc dec (see Stitch Guide) in next 2 sts] 6 times, sc in each of next 9 sc. (15 sc)

Rnd 11: [Sc in each of next 3 sc, sc dec in next 2 sc] 3 times (heel). Start to stuff with fiberfill, and continue to stuff as you go. (12 sc)

Rnds 12–34: Sc in each sc around. At end of last rnd, fasten off.

2ND LEG
Follow directions for First Leg, **changing colors** (see Stitch Guide) to leaf in last st of last rnd. Fasten off wheat.

BODY

Rnd 1: Sc in each sc around 2nd Leg, sc in each sc around First Leg, making sure both feet are pointing in same direction. *(24 sc)*

Rnd 2: Sc in **back lp** *(see Stitch Guide)* of each sc around. *(24 sc)*

Rnd 3: [Sc in next st, 2 sc in next st] around. *(36 sc)*

Rnds 4–11: Sc in each st around. Stuff with fiberfill.

Rnd 12: Working in back lps, [sc in each of next 4 sts, sc dec in next 2 sts] around. *(30 sc)*

Rnd 13: [Sc in each of next 3 sts, sc dec in next 2 sts] around. *(24 sc)*

Rnds 14–23: Sc in each st around.

Rnd 24: Working in back lps, sc in each of next 5 sts, ch 12, sc in 2nd ch from hook and in each of next 10 chs *(first strap)*, sc in each of next 17 sts of rnd 23, ch 12, sc in 2nd ch from hook and in each of next 10 chs *(2nd strap)*, sc in each of next 2 sts of rnd 23, changing to wheat in last st. Fasten off leaf.

Rnd 25: Sc in back lp only of each sc around. *(24 sc)*

Rnds 26 & 27: Sc in each st around.

Rnd 28: [Sc in each of next 2 sts, sc dec in next 2 sts] around. *(18 sc)*

Rnd 29: *Sc in each of next 5 sc, [sc dec in next 2 sc] twice, rep from * once. *(14 sc)*

Rnd 30: [Sc dec in next 2 sts] around *(neck)*. *(7 sc)*

Rnd 31: 2 sc in each st around. *(14 sc)*

Rnd 32: Rep rnd 31. *(28 sc)*

Rnds 33–40: Sc in each st around.

Rnd 41: [Sc in each of next 3 sts, sc dec in next 2 sts] 4 times, sc in each of next 8 sts. *(24 sc)*

Rnd 42: [Sc in each of next 2 sts, sc dec in next 2 sts] around. *(18 sc)*

Rnd 43: [Sc in next st, sc dec in next 2 sts] around. Leaving 5-inch end, fasten off and stuff with fiberfill. *(12 sc)*

Weave end through top of last row of sts and pull to gather top of head closed. Secure end.

TOP RUFFLE

Rnd 1: Join leaf with sc to any rem lp on rnd 24, [3 sc in next st, sl st in next st] around. Fasten off.

Rnd 2: Join honey with sc to any rem lp on rnd 25, rep rnd 1.

BOTTOM RUFFLE

Rnd 1: Join leaf with sc to any rem lp on rnd 12, sc in each st around, changing color to honey in last st. *(30 sc)*

Rnd 2: Sc in each st around, changing color to leaf in last st.

Rnd 3: [Sc in each of next 4 sc, 2 sc in next sc] around, changing color to honey in last st. *(36 sc)*

Rnd 4: [Sc in each of next 5 sc, 2 sc in next sc] around, changing color to leaf in last st. *(42 sc)*

Rnd 5: [Sc in each of next 6 sc, 2 sc in next sc] around, changing color to honey in last st. *(49 sc)*

Rnd 6: Ch 1, sc in each sc around. Fasten off.

ARM
Make 2.

Foundation rnd: With wheat, ch 2, 6 sc in 2nd ch from hook, do not join. Mark first st.

Rnd 1: Sc in each sc around. *(6 sc)*

Rnd 2: [Sc in next sc, 2 sc in next sc] around. *(9 sc)*

Rnd 3: Sc in each sc around.

Rnd 4: 2 hdc in each of next 2 sc, sc in each of next 7 sc. *(4 hdc, 7 sc)*

Rnd 5: Hdc in each of next 4 sts, sc in each of next 7 sts.

Rnd 6: [Sc dec in next 2 hdc] 2 times, sc in each of next 7 sc *(hand). (9 sc)*

Rnds 7–25: Sc in each sc around. Fill Arm with stuffing as you go, leaving last ½ inch of Arm unstuffed.

Leaving 5-inch end, fasten off. Hold edges tog. Working through both thicknesses, sew across top to close.

HAIR

Foundation rnd: With banana, ch 2, 6 sc in 2nd ch from hook, do not join. Mark first st.

Rnd 1: 2 sc in each sc around. *(12 sc)*

Rnd 2: [Sc in next st, 2 sc in next sc] around. *(18 sc)*

Rnd 3: [Sc in each of next 2 sc, 2 sc in next sc] around. *(24 sc)*

Rnd 4: [Sc in each of next 3 sc, 2 sc in next sc] around. *(30 sc)*

Rnd 5: [Sc in each of next 4 sc, 2 sc in next sc] around. *(36 sc)*

Row 6: Now working in rows, sc in next sc, hdc in next sc, dc in next sc, 2 tr in each of next 2 sc, dc in next sc, hdc in next sc, sc in each sc around, **turn.**

Row 7: Ch 1, [sc in each of next 7 sc, sc dec in next 2 sc] 3 times, leaving rem sts unworked for front, turn. *(24 sc)*

Rows 8–12: Ch 1, sc in each sc across, turn.

Row 13: Ch 1, sc dec in next 2 sc, sc in each of next 20 sc, sc dec in next 2 sc, turn.

Row 14: [Ch 10, sl st in 2nd ch from hook and in each rem ch, sl st in next sc on row 13] across. Fasten off.

FINISHING

With wheat, sew Arms to the sides of Body with thumbs pointing forward as shown in photo.

With leaf, sew straps over shoulders to back edge of bathing suit.

For face, sew 2 black beads for eyes and apply blush to cheeks as shown in photo with cotton swab.

With banana, sew Hair to head. Wrap a piece of ribbon around half the strands and tie bow, rep with rem strands.

ACCESSORIES
SUN HAT

Foundation rnd: With tangerine, ch 2, 6 sc in 2nd ch from hook, do not join. Mark first st.

Rnd 1: 2 sc in each sc around. *(12 sc)*

Rnd 2: [Sc in next st, 2 sc in next sc] around. *(18 sc)*

Rnd 3: [Sc in each of next 2 sc, 2 sc in next sc] around. *(24 sc)*

Rnd 4: [Sc in each of next 3 sc, 2 sc in next sc] around. *(30 sc)*

Rnd 5: [Sc in each of next 4 sc, 2 sc in next sc] around. *(36 sc)*

Rnd 6: Working in **back lps** *(see Stitch Guide)*, sc in each sc around.

Rnds 7 & 8: Sc in each sc around.

Rnd 9: Working in **front lps** *(see Stitch Guide)*, sc in each sc around.

Rnd 10: [Sc in each of next 5 sc, 2 sc in next sc] around. *(42 sc)*

Rnd 11: [Sc in each of next 6 sc, 2 sc in next sc] around. *(48 sc)*

Rnd 12: [Sc in each of next 7 sc, 2 sc in next sc] around. *(54 sc)*

Rnd 13: [Sc in each of next 8 sc, 2 sc in next sc] around. *(60 sc)*

Rnd 14: [Sc in each of next 9 sc, 2 sc in next sc] around. *(66 sc)*

Rnd 15: Working in back lps, sl st in each sc around. Fasten off.

FLOWER

With honey, ch 4, sl st in first ch to form ring, (ch 2, dc, ch 2, sl st) 5 times in ring. Fasten off.

FINISHING

Sew Flower to Hat. With paprika, embroider **French knot** *(see illustration)* in center of Flower.

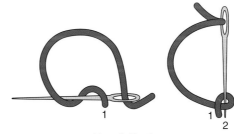

French Knot

INNER TUBE

Rnd 1: With tangerine, ch 36, being careful not to twist ch, join with sl st in 36th ch from hook to form ring, sc in each ch around, **change colors** *(see Stitch Guide)* to honey in last st. *(36 sc)*

Rnd 2: [Sc in each of next 5 sc, 2 sc in next sc] around, change to paprika in last st. *(42 sc)*

Rnd 3: [Sc in each of next 6 sc, 2 sc in next sc] around, change to tangerine in last st. *(48 sc)*

Rnd 4: [Sc in each of next 7 sc, 2 sc in next sc] around, change to honey in last st. *(54 sc)*

Rnd 5: [Sc in each of next 8 sc, 2 sc in next sc] around, change to paprika in last st. *(60 sc)*

Rnd 6: [Sc in each of next 9 sc, 2 sc in next sc] around, change to tangerine in last st. *(66 sc)*

Rnd 7: Sc in each sc around, change to honey in last st.

Rnd 8: Sc in each sc around, change to paprika in last st.

Rnd 9: Sc in each sc around, change to tangerine in last st.

Rnd 10: Sc in each sc around, change to honey in last st.

Rnd 11: [Sc in each of next 9 sc, **sc dec** *(see Stitch Guide)* in next 2 sc] around, change to paprika in last st. *(60 sc)*

Rnd 12: [Sc in each of next 8 sc, sc dec in next 2 sc] around, change to tangerine in last st. *(54 sc)*

Rnd 13: [Sc in each of next 7 sc, sc dec in next 2 sc] around, change to honey in last st. *(48 sc)*

Rnd 14: [Sc in each of next 6 sc, sc dec in next 2 sc] around, change to paprika in last st. *(42 sc)*

Rnd 15: [Sc in each of next 5 sc, sc dec in next 2 sc] around. Fasten off. *(36 sc)*

FINISHING
Sew rnd 15 to rnd 1, stuffing with fiberfill as you work.

FLIPPER
Make 2.

Rnd 1: With tangerine, ch 20, being careful not to twist ch, join with sl st in 20th ch from hook to form ring, sc in each ch around. *(20 sc)*

Rnd 2: Sc in each sc around.

Rnd 3: [Sc dec in next 2 sc, sc in each of next 8 sc] 2 times. *(18 sc)*

Rnd 4: Sc in each sc around.

Rnd 5: [Sc dec in next 2 sc, sc in each of next 7 sc] 2 times. *(16 sc)*

Rnds 6–12: Sc in each sc around.

Row 13: Now working in rows, sc in each of next 10 sc, leaving rem sts unworked, **turn**. *(10 sc)*

Rows 14–20: Ch 1, sc in each sc across, turn.

Row 21: Ch 6, leaving 5-inch end, fasten off.

FINISHING
Fold row 20 in half. Using 5-inch end, sew sts on row 20 tog to close heel. The ch-6 of row 21 will form lp at top of heel.

Flatten rnd 1 of Flipper, sew end closed. Using **straight stitch** *(see illustration)*, embroider 4 long straight stitches across top as shown in photo.

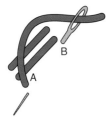

Straight Stitch

FLIP FLOP
Make 2.

SOLE SIDE
Make 2.

Rnd 1 (RS): With paprika, ch 8, sc in 2nd ch from hook, sc in each of next 5 chs, 3 sc in last ch, working in rem lps on opposite side of foundation ch, sc in each of next 5 chs, 2 sc in last ch. *(16 sc)*

Rnd 2: 2 sc in next sc, sc in each of next 5 sc, 2 sc in next sc, sc in next sc, 2 sc in next sc, sc in each of next 5 sc, 2 sc in next sc, sc in next sc. *(20 sc)*

Rnd 3: 2 sc in each of next 2 sc, sc in each of next 6 sc, 2 sc in each of next 4 sc, sc in each of next 6 sc, 2 sc in each of last 2 sc, join with sl st in first sc. Fasten off.

FINISHING
With WS facing, sew 2 Sole Sides tog.

For the straps, join paprika with sl st to side edge of Sole at toe as shown in photo, ch 15, sl st to other side edge of Sole. Fasten off. Rep for 2nd strap as shown in photo. ❖

Ginger Blue

SKILL LEVEL

INTERMEDIATE

FINISHED SIZE
Doll: Approximately 13 inches tall

MATERIALS
- Red Heart Soft Yarn medium (worsted) weight yarn (5 oz/256 yds/ 140g per ball): 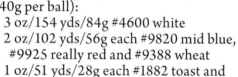 **4** MEDIUM
    - 3 oz/154 yds/84g #4600 white
    - 2 oz/102 yds/56g each #9820 mid blue, #9925 really red and #9388 wheat
    - 1 oz/51 yds/28g each #1882 toast and #9522 leaf
    - ½ oz/26 yds/14g #6768 pink
- Red Heart Soft Touch Yarn medium (worsted) weight yarn (5 oz/281 yds/140g per ball):
    - 3 oz/169 yds/84g each #4615 hot pink
- Size G/6/4mm crochet hook or size needed to obtain gauge
- Tapestry needle
- 2 small black beads
- Buttons:
    - 14 small
    - 7 medium
- Elastic ponytail holder
- 2 clear pink stickers
- Hook-and-loop fastener
- 12-inch chenille stem
- Black fabric paint
- Elastic thread
- Polyester fiberfill
- Stitch markers

GAUGE
Unstuffed: 9 sc = 2 inches; 11 sc rows = 2 inches

Stuffed: 12 sc = 3½ inches; 20 sc rows = 4 inches

PATTERN NOTES
Warning: Doll is not intended for children under 3 years of age.

When working legs, color is changed at end of every row in sequence of leaf, white, hot pink, unless otherwise stated. Carry colors not in use loosely up inside of work.

Work in continuous rounds. Do not join or turn or unless otherwise stated.

Mark first stitch of round. Move marker as work progresses.

Weave in ends as work progresses.

DOLL
FIRST LEG
Foundation rnd: With leaf, ch 2, 6 sc in 2nd ch from hook, **changing colors** (*see Stitch Guide*) to next **color in sequence** (*see Pattern Notes*) in last st, **do not join** (*see Pattern Notes*). **Mark first st** (*see Pattern Notes*).

Rnd 1: 2 sc in each st around, changing to white in last st. (*12 sc*)

Rnds 2–7: Sc in each st around, changing to next color in sequence in last st.

Rnd 8: 2 dc in each of next 3 sc, sc in each of next 9 sc, change color to next color in last st. (*6 dc, 9 sc*)

Rnd 9: 2 dc in each of next 6 dc, sc in each of next 9 sc, change color to next color in last st. (*12 dc, 9 sc*)

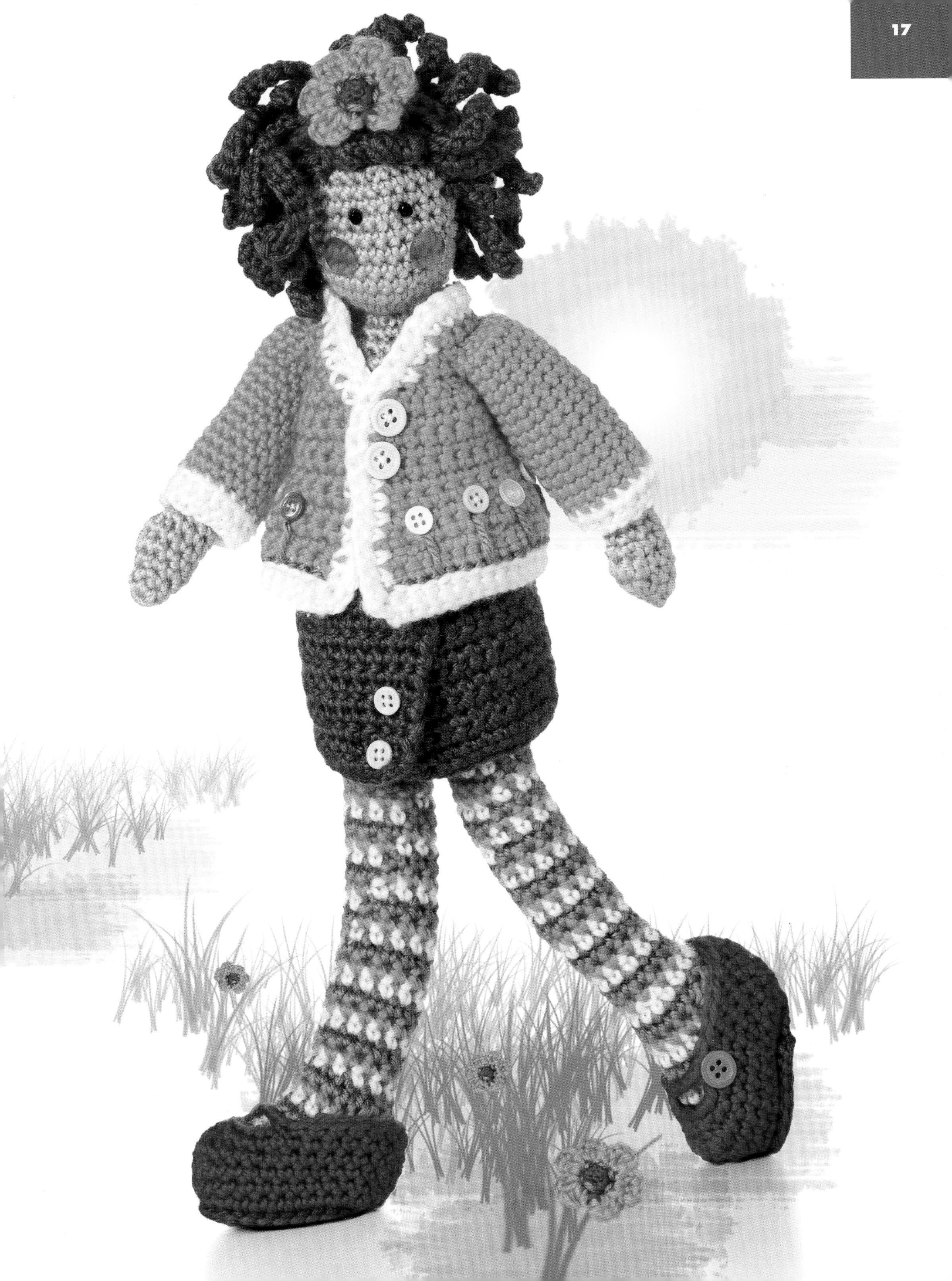

Rnd 10: [**Sc dec** (*see Stitch Guide*) in next 2 sts] 6 times, sc in each of next 9 sc. *(15 sc)*

Rnd 11: [Sc in each of next 3 sc, sc dec in next

2 sc] 3 times *(heel)*. Start to stuff with fiberfill, and continue to stuff as you go. *(12 sc)*

Rnds 12–34: Sc in each sc around following color sequence. At end of last rnd, fasten off.

2ND LEG
Follow instructions for First Leg, at end of last rnd, change color to white, **do not fasten off.** Fasten off hot pink and leaf.

BODY
Rnd 1: Sc in each sc around 2nd Leg, then sc in each sc around First Leg, making sure both toes are pointing in same direction. *(24 sc)*

Rnd 2: Sc in **back lp** (*see Stitch Guide*) only of each sc around. *(24 sc)*

Rnd 3: [Sc in next sc, 2 sc in next sc] around. *(36 sc)*

Rnds 4–11: Sc in each st around. Stuff with fiberfill.

Rnd 12: [Sc in each of next 4 sts, sc dec in next 2 sts] around. *(30 sc)*

Rnd 13: [Sc in each of next 3 sts, sc dec in next 2 sts] around. *(24 sc)*

Rnds 14–23: Sc in each st around.

Rnd 24: Sc in each of next 5 sts, ch 12, sc in 2nd ch from hook and in each of next 10 chs (*first strap*), sc in each of next 17 sts of rnd 23, ch 12, sc in 2nd ch from hook and in each of next 10 chs (*2nd strap*), sc in each of next 2 sts of rnd 23, changing to wheat in last st. Fasten off white.

Rnd 25: Working in back lps, sc in each sc around. *(24 sc)*

Rnds 26 & 27: Sc in each st around.

Rnd 28: [Sc in each of next 2 sts, sc dec in next 2 sts] around. *(18 sc)*

Rnd 29: [Sc in each of next 5 sts, sc dec in next 4 sts] twice. *(14 sc)*

Rnd 30: [Sc dec in next 2 sts] around *(neck made)*. *(7 sc)*

Rnd 31: 2 sc in each st around. *(14 sc)*

Rnd 32: Rep rnd 31. *(28 sc)*

Rnds 33–40: Sc in each st around.

Rnd 41: [Sc in each of next 3 sts, sc dec in next 2 sts] 4 times, sc in each of next 8 sts. *(24 sc)*

Rnd 42: [Sc in each of next 2 sts, sc dec in next 2 sts] around. *(18 sc)*

Rnd 43: [Sc in next st, sc dec in next 2 sts] around. Leaving 5-inch end, fasten off and stuff. *(12 sc)*

Weave end through top of sts on last row, pull to gather top of head closed. Secure end.

ARM
Make 2.

Foundation rnd: With wheat, ch 2, 6 sc in 2nd ch from hook, do not join. Mark first st.

Rnd 1: Sc in each sc around. *(6 sc)*

Rnd 2: [Sc in next sc, 2 sc in next sc] around. *(9 sc)*

Rnd 3: Sc in each sc around.

Rnd 4: 2 hdc in each of next 2 sc, sc in each of next 7 sc. *(4 hdc, 7 sc)*

Rnd 5: Hdc in each of next 4 hdc, sc in each of next 7 sc.

Rnd 6: [Sc dec in next 2 hdc] 2 times, sc in each of next 7 sc *(hand)*. *(9 sc)*

Rnds 7–25: Sc in each sc around. Fill the arm with stuffing as you go, leaving the last ½ inch of the arm unstuffed.

Leaving 5-inch end, fasten off. Hold edges tog. Working through both thicknesses, sew across top to close.

HAIR
LAYER
Make 5.

Row 1: With toast, ch 12, sc in 2nd ch from hook and in each ch across. *(11 sc)*

Row 2: [Ch 13, sc in 2nd ch from hook and in each ch across, sc in next sc] 6 times. Fasten off.

CROWN
Foundation rnd: With toast, ch 2, 6 sc in 2nd ch from hook, do not join. Mark first st.

Rnd 1: 2 sc in each sc around. *(12 sc)*

Rnd 2: [Ch 3, sc in 2nd ch from hook and in next ch, sc in next sc] 3 times *(front bangs),* [ch 13, sc in 2nd ch from hook and in each rem ch across, sc in next sc] 9 times. Fasten off.

FINISHING
Starting at base of head, sew Layers horizontally up to top of head. Sew Crown to top of head with ch-3 bangs in front.

For the face, sew 2 black beads for the eyes and fasten stickers to cheeks as shown in photo.

ACCESSORIES
SKIRT
Rnd 1: Beg at waist, with mid blue, ch 35, being careful not to twist ch, join with sl st in 35th ch from hook to form ring, ch 1, sc in each ch around. *(35 sc)*

Row 2: Now working in rows and in **front lps** (*see Stitch Guide*), sc each of next 10 sc, leaving rem sc unworked, turn. *(10 sc)*

Row 3: Ch 1, sc in each of next 35 sc, sc in rem lps in each of next 10 sc from row 2, turn. *(45 sc)*

Rows 4–15: Ch 1, sc in each of next 45 sc, turn. At end of last rnd, fasten off.

FINISHING
Sew 2 small buttons to front of Skirt. Sew elastic thread around waist of Skirt.

CARDIGAN
SLEEVE
Make 2.

Rnd 1: With white, ch 17, being careful not to twist ch, join with sl st in 17th ch from hook to form ring, ch 1, sc in each ch around. *(17 sc)*

Rnd 2: Fpsc (*see Stitch Guide*) around each sc around, **changing colors** (*see Stitch Guide*) to hot pink in last st. Fasten off white. *(17 fpsc)*

Rnd 3: Working in **back lps** (*see Stitch Guide*), sc in each fpsc around.

Rnds 4–16: Sc in each sc around. At end of last rnd, fasten off.

BODY
Row 1: With white, ch 46, sc in 2nd ch from hook and in each ch across, turn. *(45 sc)*

Row 2: Ch 1, fpsc in each sc across, changing to hot pink in last st, turn. Fasten off white. *(44 fpsc)*

Row 3: Working in **front lps** (*see Stitch Guide*), ch 1, sc in each fpsc across, turn.

Row 4: Ch 1, sc in first sc, [**sc dec** (*see Stitch Guide*) in next 2 sc, sc in each of next 4 sc] 7 times, sc in last sc, turn. *(37 sc)*

Row 5: Ch 1, sc in each sc across, turn.

Row 6: Ch 1, sc in first sc, [sc dec in next 2 sc, sc in each of next 3 sc] 7 times, sc in last sc, turn. *(30 sc)*

Rows 7–12: Ch 1, sc in each sc across, turn.

Row 13: Ch 1, [sc dec in next 2 sc] 3 times, *hold RS of Sleeve facing, working through both thicknesses of Sleeve and Body, sc in any st on last rnd of Sleeve and next st on this row, sc in each of next 2 sts on both pieces*, working on Body only, [sc dec in next 2 sts] 6 times, rep between * once to attach 2nd Sleeve, working on Body only, [sc dec in next 2 sts] 3 times, turn.

Row 14: Ch 1, sc in each of next 3 sc, sc in each of next 14 sc of Sleeve, sc in each of next 6 sc across back, sc in each of next 14 sc of Sleeve, sc in each of next 3 sc, turn. *(40 sc)*

Row 15: Ch 1, [sc dec in next 2 sc] across, turn. *(20 sc)*

Row 16: Ch 1, sc in each sc across, changing to white in last st, turn. Fasten off hot pink.

Row 17: Ch 1, sc in each of next 20 sc, working down front of Cardigan, sc in end of each of next 16 rows, turn. *(36 sc)*

Row 18: Ch 1, sc in each of next 16 sc, sc in each of next 20 sc across back, working down other

side of Cardigan, sc in end of each of next 16 rows, turn. *(52 sc)*

Row 19: Ch 1, sc in each of next 16 sc, leaving rem sts unworked. Fasten off.

FINISHING

With leaf, embroider **backstitch** *(see illustration)* across bottom edge of Cardigan, just above white border as shown in photo.

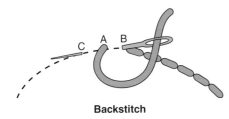

Backstitch

Using **straight stitch** *(see illustration)*, embroider 11 flower stems evenly sp around bottom of Cardigan.

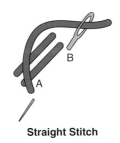

Straight Stitch

Sew small buttons to top of flower stems.

Sew 2 medium buttons to the front of the Cardigan.

Attach hook-and-loop fastener to close Cardigan.

2ND CARDIGAN

With really red, work instructions for Cardigan without changing colors.

FINISHING

Sew 3 medium buttons to front of Cardigan.

Attach hook-and-loop fastener to close Cardigan.

SHOE

Make 2.

Rnd 1: With really red, ch 9, sc in 2nd ch from

hook and in each of next 7 chs, 3 sc in last ch, working across the other side of the ch, sc in each of next 6 chs, 2 sc in last ch. *(18 sc)*

Rnd 2: [2 sc in next sc, sc in each of next 6 sc, 2 sc in next sc, sc in next sc] twice. *(22 sc)*

Rnd 3: 2 sc in each of next 2 sc, sc in each of next 8 sc, 2 sc in each of next 3 sc, sc in each of next 8 sc, 2 sc in next sc. *(28 sc)*

Rnd 4: Working in **back lps** *(see Stitch Guide)*, sc in each sc around.

Rnd 5: Hdc in each of next 3 sc, sc in each of next 10 sc, hdc in each of next 4 sc, sc in each of next 10 sc, hdc in next sc. *(8 hdc, 20 sc)*

Rnds 6 & 7: Hdc in each of next 3 hdc, sc in each of next 10 sc, hdc in each of next 4 hdc, sc in each of next 10 sc, hdc in next hdc.

Rnd 8: Hdc in each of next 3 hdc, sc in each of next 10 sc, [**sc dec** *(see Stitch Guide)* in next 2 hdc] twice, sc in each of next 10 sc, hdc in next hdc. *(4 hdc, 22 sc)*

Rnd 9: Hdc in each of next 3 hdc, sc in each of next 7 sc, ch 4, sk next 9 sc, sc in next sc. Fasten off. *(3 hdc, 8 sc)*

Rnd 10: Join toast to any unused lp in rnd 3 with sl st, sl st in each lp around rnd 3. Fasten off.

FINISHING
Sew medium button to Shoe.

HEADBAND
BAND
Join really red around ponytail holder with **sl st around ponytail holder** (*see illustration*), 35 **sc around ponytail holder** (*see illustration*), join with sl st in first sc. Fasten off.

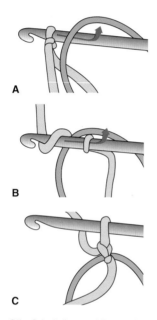

A

B

C

Slip Stitch Around Ponytail Holder

Single Crochet around band.

FLOWER
Rnd 1: With really red, ch 2, 6 sc in 2nd ch from hook, **changing color** (*see Stitch Guide*) to hot pink, join with sl st in first sc.

Rnd 2: (Ch 3, dc, ch 3, sl st) in same st as joining, sl st in next sc, [(ch 3, dc, ch 3, sl st) in next sc, sl st in next sc] 5 times. Fasten off.

FINISHING
With leaf, embroider **backstitch** (*see illustration*) around center of Flower. Sew Flower to Headband.

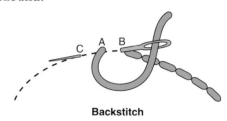

Backstitch

Embroider **French knot** (*see illustration*) in center of Flower.

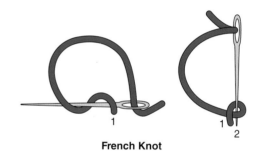

French Knot

BOOK
Make 1 each leaf, really red & mid blue.

Row 1: Ch 8, sc in 2nd ch from hook and in each ch across, turn. (*7 sc*)

Rows 2–6: Ch 1, sc in each st across, turn.

Row 7: Working in **back lps** (*see Stitch Guide*), ch 1, sc in each sc across, turn.

Row 8: Working in **front lps** (*see Stitch Guide*), ch 1, sc in each sc across, turn.

Rows 9–13: Ch 1, sc in each sc across, turn. change to white in last st of last row.

Row 14: Working in front lps, ch 1, sc in each sc across, turn.

Rows 15–19: Ch 1, sc in each sc across, turn. At end of last row, fasten off.

FINISHING

Fold Book in half with white in center. Sew Book closed. Use fabric paint to write subject on cover.

BACKPACK

Foundation rnd: With leaf, ch 2, 6 sc in 2nd ch from hook, do not join. Mark first st.

Rnd 1: 2 sc in each sc around. *(12 sc)*

Rnd 2: [Sc in next sc, 2 sc in next sc] around. *(18 sc)*

Rnd 3: [Sc in each of next 2 sc, 2 sc in next sc] around. *(24 sc)*

Rnd 4: Working in **back lps** *(see Stitch Guide),* sc in each sc around.

Rnds 5–9: Sc in each sc around.

Rnd 10: [Sc in each of next 2 sc, **sc dec** *(see Stitch Guide)* in next sc] around. *(18 sc)*

Rnds 11 & 12: Sc in each sc around.

Rnd 13: Ch 1, sc in each of next 8 sc for flap, leaving rem sts unworked, turn.

Rows 14–16: Now working in rows, ch 1, sc in each of next 8 sc, turn. At end of last row, fasten off.

POCKET

Row 1: With mid blue, ch 7, sc in 2nd ch from hook and in each ch across, turn. *(6 sc)*

Row 2: Ch 1, sc in each sc across, turn.

Row 3: Ch 1, sc dec in first 2 sc, sc in each of next 2 sc, sc dec in last 2 sc. Fasten off.

STRAP

Make 2.

With leaf, ch 16, sc in 2nd ch from hook and in each rem ch across. Fasten off. *(15 sc)*

FINISHING

Sew Pocket and Straps on to Backpack as shown in photo.

To make hanger strap, with leaf, ch 8, and fasten off. Sew strap to top of Backpack.

With leaf, using **backstitch** *(see illustration),* embroider lines on flap and pocket as shown in photo. Sew small button on top.

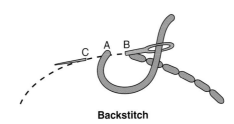

Backstitch

HANGER

Cut chenille stem to 8¾ inches. Fold over ends to cover sharp wire.

Working over chenille stem *(see illustration)*, with pink, ch 42, sc in 2nd ch from hook and in each ch across. Fasten off.

A

B

Single Crochet Over Wire

FINISHING

Sew ends closed; bend in Hanger shape as shown in photo. ❖

Nurse Deb

SKILL LEVEL
INTERMEDIATE

FINISHED SIZE
Doll: Approximately 13 inches tall

MATERIALS
- Red Heart Soft Yarn medium (worsted) weight yarn (5 oz/256 yds/ 140g per ball):
    3 oz/154 yds/84g each #9388 wheat, #4600 white and #9522 leaf
    1 oz/51 yds/28g #2515 turquoise
    ½ oz/26 yds/14g #1882 toast
- Textured medium (worsted) weight yarn:
    40 yds light brown
- Super fine (baby) weight yarn:
    30 yds off-white
- Size 10 crochet cotton
    5 yds gold
- Size G/6/4mm crochet hook or size needed to obtain gauge
- Tapestry needle
- 2 small black beads
- 4-inch piece of cardboard
- 2 clear pink stickers
- Round toothpick
- Black, blue and red markers
- 12-inch length thin beading wire
- Red seed beads
- ¼-inch white beads: 2
- ⁷⁄₁₆-inch silver button
- Polyester fiberfill
- Black fabric paint
- Stitch marker

GAUGE
Unstuffed: 9 sc = 2 inches; 11 sc rows = 2 inches
Stuffed: 12 sc = 3½ inches; 20 sc rows = 4 inches

PATTERN NOTES
Warning: Doll is not intended for children under 3 years of age.

Work in continuous rounds. Do not join or turn unless otherwise stated.

Mark first stitch of round. Move marker as work progresses.

Use wheat worsted-weight yarn unless otherwise stated.

Weave in ends as work progresses.

Join with slip stitch as indicated unless otherwise stated.

DOLL
FIRST LEG
Foundation rnd: With wheat, ch 2, 6 sc in 2nd ch from hook, **do not join** *(see Pattern Notes)*. **Mark first st** *(see Pattern Notes)*.

Rnd 1: 2 sc in each st around. *(12 sc)*

Rnds 2–7: Sc in each st around.

Rnd 8: 2 dc in each of next 3 sc, sc in each of next 9 sc. *(6 dc, 9 sc)*

Rnd 9: 2 dc in each of next 6 dc, sc in each of next 9 sc. *(12 dc, 9 sc)*

Rnd 10: [Sc dec *(see Stitch Guide)* in next 2 sts] 6 times, sc in each of next 9 sc. *(15 sc)*

Rnd 11: [Sc in each of next 3 sc, sc dec in next 2 sc] 3 times *(heel)*. Beg stuffing with fiberfill, and continue to stuff as you work. *(12 sc)*

Rnds 12–34: Sc in each sc around. At end of last rnd, fasten off.

2ND LEG
Follow instructions for First Leg, **changing colors** *(see Stitch Guide)* to **white** *(see Pattern Notes)* in last st of last rnd. Fasten off wheat.

BODY
Rnd 1: Sc in each sc around 2nd Leg, then sc in each sc around First Leg, making sure both toes are pointing in same direction. *(24 sc)*

Rnd 2: Working in **back lps** *(see Stitch Guide)*, sc in each sc around.

Rnd 3: [Sc in next st, 2 sc in next st] around. *(36 sc)*

Rnds 4–11: Sc in each st around. Stuff with fiberfill.

Rnd 12: [Sc in each of next 4 sts, sc dec in next 2 sts] around. *(30 sc)*

Rnd 13: [Sc in each of next 3 sts, sc dec in next 2 sts] around. *(24 sc)*

Rnd 14: Sc in each st around, changing to wheat in last st. Fasten off white.

Rnd 15: Working in back lps, sc in each sc around.

Rnds 16–27: Sc in each st around.

Rnd 28: [Sc in each of next 2 sts, sc dec in next 2 sts] around. *(18 sc)*

Rnd 29: *Sc in each of next 5 sts, [sc dec in next 2 sts] 2 times, rep from * once. *(14 sc)*

Rnd 30: [Sc dec in next 2 sts] around *(neck)*. *(7 sc)*

Rnd 31: 2 sc in each st around. *(14 sc)*

Rnd 32: Rep rnd 31. *(28 sc)*

Rnds 33–40: Sc in each st around.

Rnd 41: [Sc in each of next 3 sts, sc dec in next 2 sts] 4 times, sc in each of next 8 sts. *(24 sc)*

Rnd 42: [Sc in each of next 2 sts, sc dec in next 2 sts] around. *(18 sc)*

Rnd 43: [Sc in next st, sc dec in next 2 sts] around. Leaving 5-inch end, fasten off and stuff. *(12 sc)*

Weave long end through top of last rnd of sts, pull to gather top of head closed. Secure end.

ARM
Make 2.

Foundation rnd: With wheat, ch 2, 6 sc in 2nd ch from hook, do not join. Mark first st.

Rnd 1: Sc in each st around. *(6 sc)*

Rnd 2: [Sc in next st, 2 sc in next st] around. *(9 sc)*

Rnd 3: Sc in each st around.

Rnd 4: 2 hdc in each of next 2 sts, sc in each of next 7 sts. *(4 hdc, 7 sc)*

Rnd 5: Hdc in each of next 4 sts, sc in each of next 7 sts.

Rnd 6: [Sc dec in next 2 sts] 2 times, sc in each of next 7 sts *(hand)*. *(9 sc)*

Rnds 7–25: Sc in each sc around. Fill Arm with stuffing as you go, leaving last ½ inch of Arm unstuffed.

Leaving 5-inch end, fasten off. Hold edges tog. Working through both thicknesses, sew across top to close.

HAIR
With textured yarn, wrap yarn 135 times around cardboard. Cut lps on 1 side only.

Start at the neck and work, row by row, upward toward crown, tie yarn pieces around each individual st and knot. Trim as needed.

FINISHING

With wheat, sew Arms to sides of Body as shown in photo with thumbs pointing forward.

For the face, sew 2 black beads for the eyes and fasten stickers to cheeks as shown in photo.

ACCESSORIES
SHIRT

Foundation rnd: With leaf, ch 42, **join** *(see Pattern Notes)* in 42nd ch from hook to form ring.

Rnd 1: Ch 1, sc in same ch as join, sc in each rem ch around. *(42 sc)*

Rnds 2 & 3: Sc in each sc around.

Rnd 4: [Sc in each of next 5 sc, sc dec in next 2 sc] around. *(36 sc)*

Rnd 5: Sc in each sc around.

Rnd 6: [Sc in each of next 4 sc, sc dec in next 2 sc] around. *(30 sc)*

Rnds 7–12: Sc in each sc around.

Row 13 (RS): Now working in rows, sc in each of next 12 sc, leaving rem sts unworked, turn.

Rows 14–19: Ch 1, sc in each sc across, turn. Fasten off after last row *(back)*. *(12 sc)*

Row 20: With RS facing, sk next 2 sc on rnd 12, join in next sc, sc in same sc as join, sc in each of next 6 sc, turn. *(7 sc)*

Row 21: Ch 1, **sc dec** *(see Stitch Guide)* in next 2 sc, sc in each of next 5 sc, leaving rem sc unworked, turn. *(6 sc)*

Row 22: Ch 1, sc in each of next 4 sc, sc dec in next 2 sc, turn. *(5 sc)*

Row 23: Ch 1, sc dec in next 2 sc, sc in each of next 3 sc, turn. *(6 sc)*

Row 24: Ch 1, sc in each of next 2 sc, sc dec in next 2 sc. Fasten off *(left side)*. *(5 sc)*

Row 25: With RS facing, join in next sc on rnd 12, sc dec in same st as join and next sc, sc in each of next 5 sc, turn. *(6 sc)*

Row 26: Ch 1, sc in each of next 4 sc, sc dec in next 2 sc, turn. *(5 sc)*

Row 27: Ch 1, sc dec in next 2 sc, sc in each of next 3 sc, turn. *(4 sc)*

Row 28: Ch 1, sc in each of next 2 sc, sc dec in next 2 sc, turn. *(3 sc)*

Row 29: Ch 1, sc in each sc across. Fasten off *(right side).*

FINISHING
Sew shoulder seams tog.

SLEEVE
Rnd 1: Join leaf in armhole, evenly sp 13 sc around armhole, join in first sc.

Rnds 2–5: Sc in each sc around. At end of last rnd, fasten off.

Rep Sleeve on rem armhole.

POCKET
Make 3.

Row 1: With leaf, ch 4, sc in 2nd ch from hook, sc in each ch across, turn. *(3 sc)*

Rows 2–4: Ch 1, sc in each sc across. At end of last row, leaving 8-inch end, fasten off.

FINISHING
Sew 1 Pocket to front of shirt. Rem 2 Pockets will be used on Pants.

For the pens, break toothpick in half and trim as needed. Color with markers and insert in pocket.

PANTS
Row 1: With leaf, ch 60. Fasten off.

Row 2: Sk 14 chs, join leaf in next ch, sc in each of next 30 chs, turn. *(30 sc)*

Row 3: Ch 1, sc in each sc across, turn.

Row 4: Ch 1, [sc in each of next 4 sc, 2 sc in next sc] 6 times, turn. *(36 sc)*

Row 5: Ch 1, sc in each sc across, turn.

Row 6: Ch 1, sc in each sc across, sl st in first sc.

Rnds 7–15: Now working in rnds, ch 1, sc in each sc around, join in first sc.

Rnd 16: To form Pant legs, ch 1, sc in each of next 9 sc, sk next 18 sc, sc in each of next 9 sc, join in first sc. *(18 sc)*

Rnds 17–39: Ch 1, sc in each sc around, join in first sc. At end of last rnd, fasten off.

Rnd 40: Join leaf with sc in first sk st of rnd 16, sc in each sk sc around, join in first sc. *(18 sc)*

Rnds 41–63: Ch 1, sc in each sc around, join in first sc. At end of last rnd, fasten off.

FINISHING
Sew opening in crotch closed.

Sew rem 2 Pockets to back of Pants.

SHOE
Make 2.

Foundation rnd: With turquoise, ch 2, 6 sc in 2nd ch from hook, do not join. Mark first st.

Rnd 1: 2 sc in each sc around. *(12 sc)*

Rnd 2: [Sc in next sc, 2 sc in next sc] around. *(18 sc)*

Rnd 3: [Sc in next sc, ch 2, sk next sc] 2 times, sc in each of next 14 sc. *(16 sc)*

Rnd 4: [Sc in next sc, sc in next ch-2 sp] 2 times, sc in each of next 14 sc. *(18 sc)*

Rnd 5: [Sc in next sc, ch 2, sk next sc] 2 times, sc in each of next 14 sc. *(16 sc)*

Rnd 6: [Sc in next sc, sc in next ch-2 sp] 2 times, sc in each of next 14 sc, turn. *(18 sc)*

Row 7: Now working in rows, sc in each of next 12 sc, leaving rem sc unworked, **turn**. *(12 sc)*

Rows 8–12: Ch 1, sc in each of next 12 sc, turn.

Row 13: Ch 1, [sc dec in next 2 sc] 6 times, turn. *(6 sc)*

Row 14: Ch 1, [sc dec in next 2 sc] 3 times, sl st around entire Shoe opening. Fasten off.

STETHOSCOPE

1. Attach 1 white bead *(ear piece)* to 1 end of beading wire. Twist to secure.

2. Thread 45 red seed beads on wire, or enough beads as needed to measure 3¼ inches. Add silver button to wire.

3. Thread wire back up through 16 beads.

4. Thread 29 more beads on wire. Thread on rem white bead. Twist to secure and thread wire back down 6 or 7 red beads.

5. Cut wire. Twist Stethoscope into shape. Hang around Doll's neck.

CHART
BOARD
Row 1: With toast, ch 10, sc in 2nd ch from hook,

sc in each ch across, turn. *(9 sc)*

Rows 2–8: Ch 1, sc in each sc across, turn. At end of last row, fasten off.

PAPER
Row 1: With white, ch 9, sc in 2nd ch from hook, sc in each ch across, turn. *(8 sc)*

Rows 2–6: Ch 1, sc in each sc across, turn. At end of last row, fasten off.

METAL CLIP
Row 1: With gold, ch 7, sc in 2nd ch from hook, sc in each ch across, turn. *(6 sc)*

Rows 2 & 3: Ch 1, sc in each sc across, turn. At end of last row, fasten off.

FINISHING
Sew Paper to Board.

Sew Clip to Chart.

Use fabric paint to write "Birth Wt." on Paper.

BABY
Foundation rnd: With wheat, ch 2, 6 sc in 2nd ch from hook, do not join. Mark first st.

Rnd 1: 2 sc in each sc around. *(12 sc)*

Rnds 2–10: Sc in each sc around. At end of last rnd, leaving long end, fasten off and stuff. Weave end through top of sts on last row. Pull to gather bottom closed. Secure end.

BABY BLANKET
Row 1: With off-white baby yarn, ch 25, dc in 3rd ch from hook and in each ch across, turn. *(23 dc)*

Rows 2–12: Ch 2 *(counts as first dc)*, dc in each dc across, turn. At end of last row, fasten off.

FINISHING
Wrap Baby in Blanket, stitch to secure.

Add 2 small dots of blue marker for eyes.

Sew Baby to Doll's arms. ❖

STITCH GUIDE

STITCH ABBREVIATIONS

beg ....begin/begins/beginning
bpdc ....back post double crochet
bpsc ....back post single crochet
bptr ....back post treble crochet
CC ....contrasting color
ch(s) ....chain(s)
ch- ....refers to chain or space
    previously made (i.e., ch-1 space)
ch sp(s) ....chain space(s)
cl(s) .... cluster(s)
cm ....centimeter(s)
dc ....double crochet (singular/plural)
dc dec ....double crochet 2 or more
    stitches together, as indicated
dec .... decrease/decreases/decreasing
dtr .... double treble crochet
ext ....extended
fpdc ....front post double crochet
fpsc .... front post single crochet
fptr .... front post treble crochet
g ....gram(s)
hdc ....half double crochet
hdc dec ....half double crochet 2 or more
    stitches together, as indicated
inc ....increase/increases/increasing
lp(s) ....loop(s)
MC ....main color
mm ....millimeter(s)
oz ....ounce(s)
pc ....popcorn(s)
rem ....remain/remains/remaining
rep(s) ....repeat(s)
rnd(s) ....round(s)
RS ....right side
sc ....single crochet (singular/plural)
sc dec ....single crochet 2 or more
    stitches together, as indicated
sk ....skip/skipped/skipping
sl st(s) .... slip stitch(es)
sp(s) ....space(s)/spaced
st(s) ....stitch(es)
tog ....together
tr...treble crochet
trtr ....triple treble
WS .... wrong side
yd(s) ....yard(s)
yo ....yarn over

YARN CONVERSION

OUNCES TO GRAMS		GRAMS TO OUNCES	
1	28.4	25	7⁄8
2	56.7	40	1²⁄₃
3	85.0	50	1¾
4	113.4	100	3½

UNITED STATES		UNITED KINGDOM
sl st (slip stitch)	=	sc (single crochet)
sc (single crochet)	=	dc (double crochet)
hdc (half double crochet)	=	htr (half treble crochet)
dc (double crochet)	=	tr (treble crochet)
tr (treble crochet)	=	dtr (double treble crochet)
dtr (double treble crochet)	=	ttr (triple treble crochet)
skip	=	miss

Single crochet decrease (sc dec):
(Insert hook, yo, draw lp through) in each of the sts indicated, yo, draw through all lps on hook.

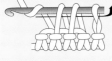

Example of 2-sc dec

Half double crochet decrease (hdc dec):
(Yo, insert hook, yo, draw lp through) in each of the sts indicated, yo, draw through all lps on hook.

Example of 2-hdc dec

Reverse single crochet (reverse sc):
Ch 1, sk first st, working from left to right, insert hook in next st from front to back, draw up lp on hook, yo, and draw through both lps on hook.

Chain (ch):
Yo, pull through lp on hook.

Single crochet (sc):
Insert hook in st, yo, pull through st, yo, pull through both lps on hook.

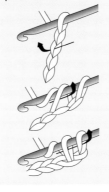

Double crochet (dc):
Yo, insert hook in st, yo, pull through st, [yo, pull through 2 lps] twice.

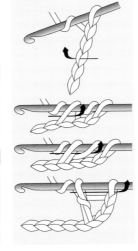

Double crochet decrease (dc dec):
(Yo, insert hook, yo, draw lp through, yo, draw through 2 lps on hook) in each of the sts indicated, yo, draw through all lps on hook.

Example of 2-dc dec

Front loop (front lp) Back loop (back lp)

Front Loop   Back Loop

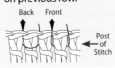

Front post stitch (fp): Back post stitch (bp):
When working post st, insert hook from right to left around post of st on previous row.

Back   Front

Post of Stitch

Half double crochet (hdc):
Yo, insert hook in st, yo, pull through st, yo, pull through all 3 lps on hook.

Double treble crochet (dtr):
Yo 3 times, insert hook in st, yo, pull through st, [yo, pull through 2 lps] 4 times.

Treble crochet decrease (tr dec):
Holding back last lp of each st, tr in each of the sts indicated, yo, pull through all lps on hook.

Example of 2-tr dec

Slip stitch (sl st):
Insert hook in st, pull through both lps on hook.

Chain color change (ch color change)
Yo with new color, draw through last lp on hook.

Double crochet color change (dc color change)
Drop first color, yo with new color, draw through last 2 lps of st.

Treble crochet (tr):
Yo twice, insert hook in st, yo, pull through st, [yo, pull through 2 lps] 3 times.

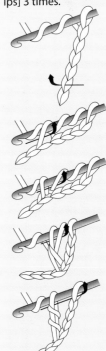

Metric Conversion Charts

METRIC CONVERSIONS

yards	x	.9144	=	metres (m)
yards	x	91.44	=	centimetres (cm)
inches	x	2.54	=	centimetres (cm)
inches	x	25.40	=	millimetres (mm)
inches	x	.0254	=	metres (m)

centimetres	x	.3937	=	inches
metres	x	1.0936	=	yards

INCHES INTO MILLIMETRES & CENTIMETRES (Rounded off slightly)

inches	mm	cm	inches	cm	inches	cm	inches	cm
1/8	3	0.3	5	12.5	21	53.5	38	96.5
1/4	6	0.6	5 1/2	14	22	56	39	99
3/8	10	1	6	15	23	58.5	40	101.5
1/2	13	1.3	7	18	24	61	41	104
5/8	15	1.5	8	20.5	25	63.5	42	106.5
3/4	20	2	9	23	26	66	43	109
7/8	22	2.2	10	25.5	27	68.5	44	112
1	25	2.5	11	28	28	71	45	114.5
1 1/4	32	3.2	12	30.5	29	73.5	46	117
1 1/2	38	3.8	13	33	30	76	47	119.5
1 3/4	45	4.5	14	35.5	31	79	48	122
2	50	5	15	38	32	81.5	49	124.5
2 1/2	65	6.5	16	40.5	33	84	50	127
3	75	7.5	17	43	34	86.5		
3 1/2	90	9	18	46	35	89		
4	100	10	19	48.5	36	91.5		
4 1/2	115	11.5	20	51	37	94		

KNITTING NEEDLES CONVERSION CHART

Canada/U.S.	0	1	2	3	4	5	6	7	8	9	10	10½	11	13	15
Metric (mm)	2	2¼	2¾	3¼	3½	3¾	4	4½	5	5½	6	6½	8	9	10

CROCHET HOOKS CONVERSION CHART

Canada/U.S.	1/B	2/C	3/D	4/E	5/F	6/G	8/H	9/I	10/J	10½/K	N
Metric (mm)	2.25	2.75	3.25	3.5	3.75	4.25	5	5.5	6	6.5	9.0

Annie's® *Crochet Your Own Dolls & Accessories* is published by Annie's, 306 East Parr Road, Berne, IN 46711. Printed in USA. Copyright © 2012, 2013 Annie's. All rights reserved. This publication may not be reproduced in part or in whole without written permission from the publisher.

RETAIL STORES: If you would like to carry this pattern book or any other Annie's publications, visit AnniesWSL.com.

Every effort has been made to ensure that the instructions in this pattern book are complete and accurate. We cannot, however, take responsibility for human error, typographical mistakes or variations in individual work. Please visit AnniesCustomerCare.com to check for pattern updates.

ISBN: 978-1-59635-481-4

2 3 4 5 6 7 8 9